CARDS AND WRAPPINGS

Vivienne Bolton

PARRAGON

Editor
Barbara Segall

Art Direction
Full Steam Ahead

Design Team
Design Study

Photography
Patrick Spillane

Photographic Co-ordinator
Liz Spillane

Styling
Bianca Boulton

Project Management
Kate Miles

The publishers would like to thank Inscribe Ltd., Bordon, Hants. for
providing the art materials used in these projects and
Sophie Boulton for her assistance.

First published in 1998 by
Parragon
13 Whiteladies Road, Clifton, Bristol
BS8 1PB

24681097531

Produced by Miles Kelly Publishing Ltd
Unit 11, Bardfield Centre, Great Bardfield, Essex CM7 4SL

British Library Cataloguing-in-Publication Data
A catalogue record for this book is available from the British Library.

ISBN 0-75253-052-6

Printed in Italy

GET CRAFTY

CARDS AND WRAPPINGS

Contents

Sticker Fun

Decorating writing paper is a great way to make good use of a sticker collection. Stickers come in such a wide range of colours and styles, you could customize writing paper to suit almost every hobby or lifestyle. Choose brightly coloured writing paper to decorate and find matching envelopes. Use a large sheet of paper to make a folder for holding your matching writing paper and envelopes. You will always be able to find them when you need to send a letter.

You will need:

Coloured paper

A selection of stickers

1 Choose brightly coloured writing paper to make good use of the stickers. These rainbow stickers look stylish centred at the top of the page.

2 Decorate the envelopes with a sticker on the bottom left hand corner. You could co-ordinate your paper and envelopes using two colours.

3 To make a folder to hold your decorated paper, fold up a large sheet of thin card, three-quarters the length of the card, leaving a piece to fold down into a flap.

4 Hold the sides together with colourful stickers and decorate the front of the folder with matching stickers.

Gift Boxes

Surprise your friends with one of these stylish hand made boxes. Make small boxes from paper or slightly larger boxes from thin card. A double layer of wrapping paper would make an attractive box. Use paper that suits the gift and make a box from flowery paper to hold packets of seeds or use red paper for a Valentine box. Plain paper can be decorated with stickers or coloured tape. Try decorating paper first with crayons or pencils. A set of boxes could be used to hold cake and party favours and you could personalize the boxes with your guests' names. Once you have mastered the method you will find the boxes quick and easy to make.

You will need:
Paper

Ruler

Scissors

Glue

1 Fold a rectangular piece of paper in half.

2 Fold each half in on itself, so that both ends meet in the middle.

3 With the paper opened out, you will see crease marks like this.

4 Now fold the paper into thirds in the opposite direction to your first folds.

5 Now the creases should look like this.

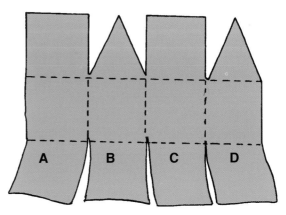

6 Cut along the crease lines and cut out the triangles as shown in the picture above.

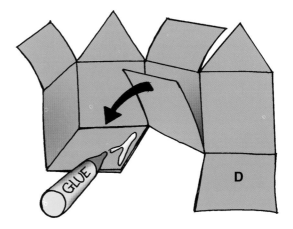

7 Fold in and glue flap B onto flap A, flap C onto flap B and flap D onto flap C. Finally stick the open edge with sticky tape on the inside and make a hole at the top of both triangles for a ribbon.

Pop-up Cards

This pop-up card is simple to make and will brighten up someone's day. When placed on a windowsill or mantlepiece it will look as if a bunch of flowers is bursting out of the card. The cards are made and decorated with thin card. If you don't have any coloured thin card available, use card from a cereal packet and paint it in bright colours yourself.

You will need:

Coloured thin card

Scissors

Glue

Coloured paper

Felt tips pens

1 Begin by folding a sheet of thin card in half and then open it out. Cut out a small square of card and fold it in half. Fold a lip on the two edges, and glue these into the card to make the vase. Open and close the card to check the vase flattens when you close it.

2 Using green thin card, cut the stalks and leaves, use glue to attach these to the inside of the vase. Cut out some tulip-shaped flowers and glue them onto the stalks, making sure that they are hidden when the card is closed.

3 Cut small heart shapes to decorate the vase from red paper, folded over.

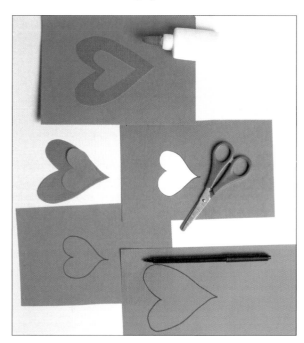

4 Now decorate the front of the card with a large red heart and a smaller blue heart, to match the rest of the design. Now you are ready to write your message on the card, using felt tip pens.

When trying out something for the first time, start by making a rough example out of scrap paper and card.

Bows & Ribbons

Bows and ribbons provide the final touch to a beautifully wrapped gift. You can decorate plain ribbon with felt tip pens, creating your own designs. The ribbons shown here are decorated with tiny motor vehicles and balloons, but any design would be fun. Hallowe'en pumpkins or Christmas trees are bright and easy to draw. Bows are quick to make using the method shown. Choose thin ribbon to make small bows and wider ribbon for larger bows. Co-ordinate the patterns and colours of your home made bows with wrapping paper for a stylish look.

You will need:

Ribbon

Felt tip pens

Ruler

Scissors

Needle and thread

1 Use felt tip pens to decorate plain ribbon. Cut a little ribbon off to practise on. Press the pen down gently to prevent the colour bleeding across the weave of the ribbon.

Complete the use of one colour before moving on to the next. Remember to repeat your pattern to give the ribbon a shop bought look.

2 Spread a 60cm length of ribbon across the work surface. Use a felt tip pen and ruler to make a tiny mark every 6cm. Thread the needle with thread about 20cm longer than the ribbon and make a good knot at the end. Sew a small stitch at each mark on the ribbon. Now pull gently at the thread and the ribbon should bunch up, making a fancy bow.

PAPER
Printed Cards

Spend a rainy afternoon making potato cuts to print with and you will be able to set up a production line and make a collection of cards or writing paper. The fish card is made with layers of different coloured paper, each slightly smaller than the other. Biscuit cutters come in lots of shapes and provide a quick way to make home made stamps. Use a small rabbit shape to decorate writing paper and envelopes. The bunch of carrots is made by first drawing the shape onto the potato half, then cutting it out with a knife. A set of cards tied with matching ribbon would make a good gift.

You will need:
A potato

Biscuit cutters

Knife

Paint and saucer

Sponge

Paper

1 Begin by cutting a potato in half. Take the fish-shaped biscuit cutter and press it firmly into the flesh of one half of the potato. Use the knife to cut around the shape. Lift off the cutter and remove the excess potato flesh. Put a little paint onto a saucer and use the sponge to evenly distribute the paint on the stamp. Now press the stamp gently onto blue paper. Print a few fish and leave them to dry.

2 Take a white sheet of paper and fold it in half to make the card. Now take a square of blue paper slightly smaller than the card and glue it on the front. Next glue on a small piece of gold paper. Cut out the fish print and glue it on top.

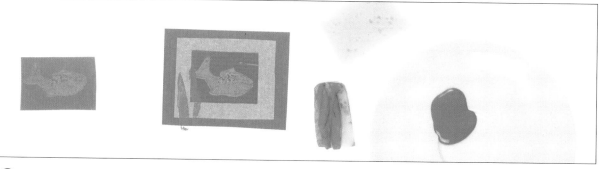

3 To finish off the picture you will need to make a simple stamp from the other half of the potato. Use the knife to cut a weed shape. Spread green paint on the stamp and print leaves of seaweed onto the card. Leave to dry.

Protect your work surface with newspaper or a plastic cloth before you begin.

It is a good idea to practise stamping your design on some scrap paper to get an idea of how much paint you need to apply to the stamp.

Concertina Cards

Make one of these cards and watch the concertina movement when you open and close the card. The clown gives a good impression of playing his concertina, and the ballerina's tutu stands proudly out. The poodle's ruff looks almost real! The cards are quite simple to make, so think up some ideas of your own. You could use the concertina shape to make a bumble bee's body, or maybe a wriggly worm holding an umbrella! Use a little imagination and some brightly coloured paper to create a novel concertina card for a friend's birthday.

1 Fold a sheet of paper in half to form the card. Use the ruler to measure where to fix the concertina ends. Mark the two points, which should be evenly spaced on either side of the central fold.

4 You will need to cut a long narrow strip of yellow paper to make the concertina. Fold it to form a fan. When folding paper always use your thumbnail to press the fold firmly down.

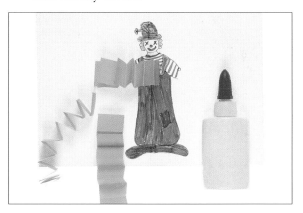

2 Draw the clown with the arms ending at the dots. Make the picture quite simple.

5 Use glue to attach each end of the concertina to the end of the clown's arms.

3 Colour in your picture with bright shades, making it as attractive as possible.

You will need:

Paper

Ruler

Felt tip pens

Scissors

Glue

PAPER AND RIBBON
Gift Bags

P ack your Christmas gifts in these brightly coloured paper bags. You can make them almost any size. Use one layer of paper for smaller bags and a double layer to make larger bags. You could decorate the paper before you begin. Make a stencil to decorate the paper if you are making a lot of bags all to match for party favours. The bag handles can be made from string or pretty ribbon. Have a look around for paper decorated on both sides, or use gold or silver paper.

You will need:
A selection of paper

Glue

Hole punch

Ribbon

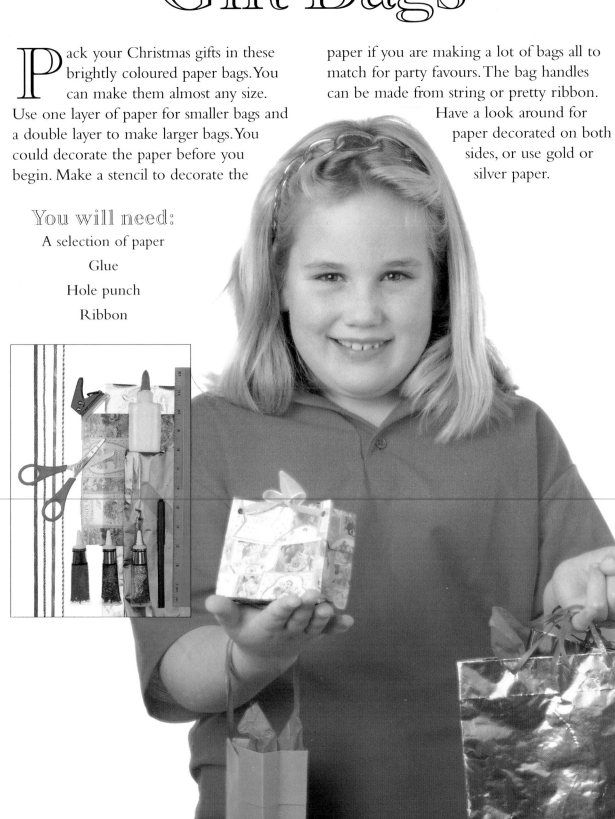

1 Begin by folding the paper in by about one quarter of its length. Run your thumbnail along the fold to mark it well.

2 Turn the folded sheet of paper over and apply glue to one end.

3 Glue the edges together to form a cylinder shape. Allow the glue to dry.

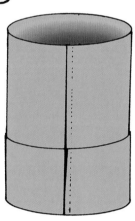

4 Flatten the cylinder shape. Run your thumbnail along the edges to make a good fold.

5 Fold about one quarter over on each side.

6 Open the two folds and press them inwards. You should now have a bag shape.

7 Make a fold upwards to form the base of the bag. Glue it down.

8 Use a hole punch to make holes to thread a ribbon through and make a handle.

CARD AND PAPER
Cut-out Cards

Make a row of paper flowerpots and turn them into a birthday card, or a row of blue and white teapots to send as an invitation to tea. The Christmas tree cards can be decorated as brightly as you wish and the colourful fish swimming around in their bowls will brighten up the mantlepiece. Cut-out cards are quick and easy to make and decorate. When choosing the shape remember that the card will need to be cut out so draw a compact picture. A Christmas tree cut from plain white paper and decorated using a gold pen would be very stylish.

You will need:

Paper

Felt tip pens

Crayons

Scissors

Glue

Sequins to decorate

When decorating your cards try outlining coloured-in pictures with a darker shade. This will accentuate the shapes and give the cards a professional finish.

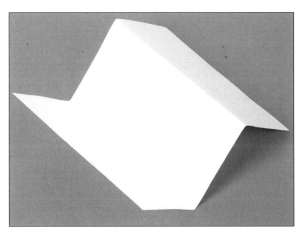

1 This card is easy to make and fun to colour, you will need a rectangle of plain white paper. Fold the sheet of paper in three to make the card shape

4 Colour in your card using bright shades.

2 On the front of the card draw a pot of flowers. Make sure the flower pots are joined at the lip, or the card will fall apart when you cut it out.

5 To make this cheery Christmas card use a sheet of green paper folded in three. Draw on the Christmas tree shape and cut it out. Take care to leave the branches joined together at the base of the tree. Glue on small flowerpots cut from paper for the trees to stand in and decorate the Christmas trees with sequins and shiny stars, glued on.

3 Cut away the excess paper.

Notepaper

Fancy writing paper makes letterwriting more fun. You can decorate paper to suit the season: make bright sunny pictures for summer holiday letters and snowy scenes for winter times. You may like to experiment with other ideas. Maybe a seaside scene or some rolling hills covered in tiny black sheep and cows would suit a holiday mood. Choose bright co-ordinated colours and matching envelopes. Use the steely glints of shiny gold or silver pens to create a night scene or even to decorate a set of paper with a firework display.

You will need:

Paper

Felt tip pens

Scissors

Glue

1 This summery style is made from green, blue and white sheets of paper. Decorate the sky-blue sheet of paper first. Cut out small fluffy white clouds and glue them onto the sky.

3 This snowscene is decorated with a cheerful looking snowman. Draw the snowman onto a white sheet of paper. Remember to draw the horizon onto the page.

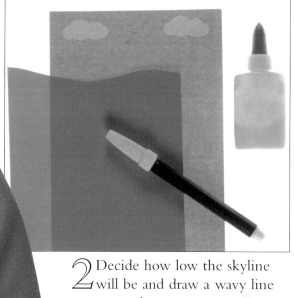

2 Decide how low the skyline will be and draw a wavy line across the green paper. Cut away the excess paper to leave grassy green hills. Lay one piece of paper on top of the other to create the scene.

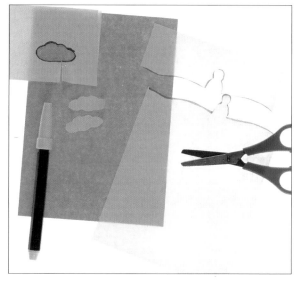

4 Use scissors to cut out the snowman and lay the sheet of white paper onto the blue sky. Decorate the snowman using a black felt tip pen, giving him a cheerful smile.

PAPER
Envelopes

You might have difficulty finding envelopes that are the correct size, especially if they are to match the paper and cards you have designed. Don't worry – there is no problem. Use these simple instructions and make envelopes to fit almost every size and shape of card. You could make the envelope from matching paper, patterned wrapping paper (you will need to attach a plain label for the address) or recycled paper. Decorate your home made envelopes using felt tip pens, stickers, paint or crayons. Remember to make the card first and use it to work around.

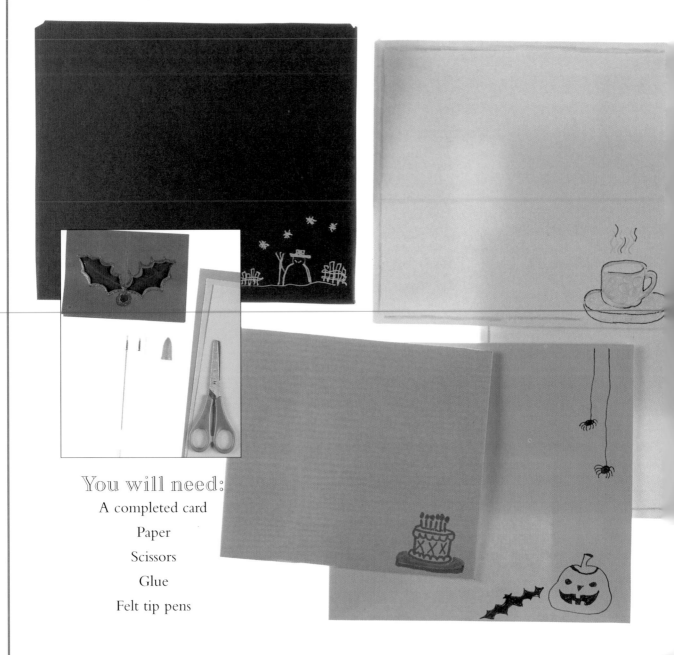

You will need:
A completed card
Paper
Scissors
Glue
Felt tip pens

1 Place the card in the centre of the paper. Fold the paper up, over the card.

2 Fold the envelope flap down, over the card.

3 Fold in the sides. Make sure the card fits the folded shape comfortably.

4 Cut away the excess paper from the front of the envelope.

5 Cut a flap shape.

6 Use glue to hold the envelope in shape.

CARD AND PAPER
Silhouettes

Making silhouettes was once a popular pastime. People would cut silhouettes in all sorts of shapes, profile outlines being very popular. Fine cutting skills are needed to make silhouettes. Practise on scraps of paper to learn the technique before you set to work on these shapes. Cut your silhouette from black paper and lay it on a light background. Try your hand at a larger silhouette, maybe a profile of yourself or a friend, to frame and hang on your bedroom wall. Silhouettes of candles and Christmas puddings are very seasonal, while the pumpkin and cat cut-outs would make good Hallowe'en party invitations.

You will need:
Paper

Wax or pencil crayon

Scissors

Glue

1 Fold a sheet of black paper in half. Draw half a butterfly on to one side of the folded shape. Cut it out. It is possible to cut out the butterfly shape freehand.

Make a card from a folded sheet of paper and glue a piece of red paper onto the cover of the card. Glue the butterfly silhouette onto the piece of red paper.

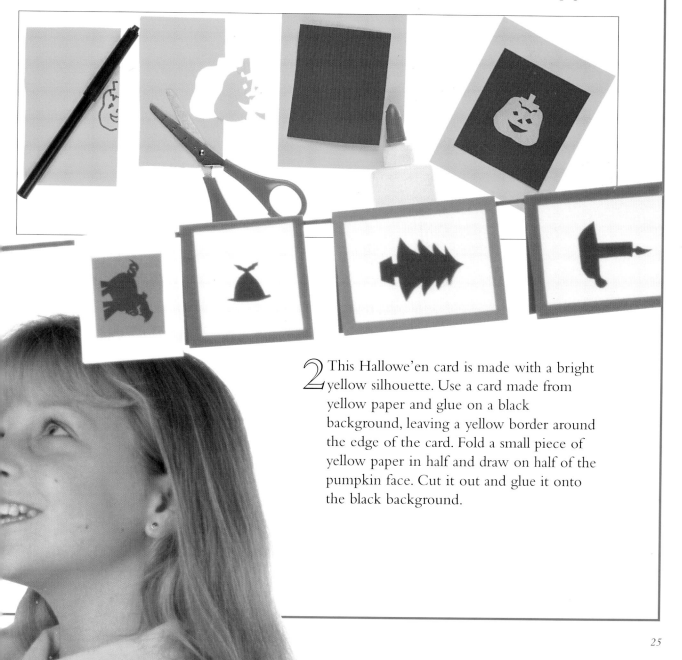

2 This Hallowe'en card is made with a bright yellow silhouette. Use a card made from yellow paper and glue on a black background, leaving a yellow border around the edge of the card. Fold a small piece of yellow paper in half and draw on half of the pumpkin face. Cut it out and glue it onto the black background.

Stained Glass

Create your own stained glass pictures with coloured plastic wrapping. Placed where the light shines through them these cards are most effective. Coloured wrapping film is available from craft shops, however you might want to save sweet wrappers and keep an eye out for coloured clear plastic to recycle. The holly leaves make a good Christmas card. You can have fun decorating the card with coloured glitter glue.

You will need:

Black paper

Felt tip pen

Scissors

Coloured clear wrapping

Glue and glitter glue

1 To make this clear blue fish bowl card begin by folding a sheet of white paper in half. Draw on a simple fish bowl shape and cut it out.

2 Cut a rectangle of blue coloured wrapping slightly larger than the fish bowl. Glue the rectangle onto the inside of the card, covering the fish bowl shape. Fold the card closed. You will decorate the cover of the card.

3 Use glitter glue to fill the bowl with fish, coloured seaweed and pebbles. Don't forget to paint on air bubbles. Decorate the edge of the bowl as well.

4 You will need a sheet of black paper folded in half to make the holly card. Begin by cutting out the holly leaves and berries. Cut green coloured wrapping slightly larger than the cut-out leaves and glue it to the inside of the card. Use red wrapping for the berries. Fold the card to close it and decorate the stained glass-effect card with coloured glitter glue.

If you do not have glitter glue, make your own. Use PVA glue and mix in an equal amount of fine glitter. Use a fine paint-brush to apply the glitter glue to your model or card.

TISSUE PAPER
Stencilled Wrapping Paper

Stencilling is a quick and effective way to decorate wrapping paper and gift tags. Use gold or silver paint to turn plain tissue paper into expensive looking wrapping paper. The stencils are easily cut from small sheets of paper folded in half. You could make matching gift wrap and tags to suit any event or gift. Once you have mastered the art of stencilling you may want to try using two colours. It is also useful to remember that other colouring materials and methods are good for stencilling. You don't have to use paint, try wax crayons for example.

You will need:

Paper

Pencil

Scissors

Tissue paper

Paint

Saucer

Sponge

Hole punch

Thread

Always protect your work surface with newspaper or a vinyl cloth.

Remember to wipe up any spills as they happen. A good craftsperson leaves a tidy work surface.

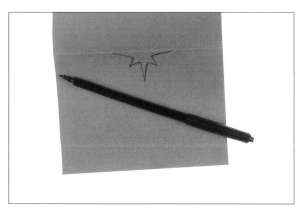

1 To make a stencil you will need a small sheet of paper. Fold it in half and draw on half of the picture, in this case half of the star, as shown in the picture above.

2 Use the scissors to cut the star out, taking care not to leave any jagged edges and not to cut into the paper. If you do, the stencil paint may come through.

3 Spread a sheet of tissue paper across your work surface. Pour a little paint onto the saucer, spread it on the sponge, damping the sponge down. Place the stencil on some rough paper and practise until you are confident.

4 Stencil on the stars taking care not to smudge the paint when you lift the stencil off the paper. Hang your stencilled paper up to dry. It is a good idea to make quite a few sheets at a time, as well as matching gift tags.

5 Use paper to make these matching gift tags. Cut them out with scissors. Stencil on the star and leave to dry.

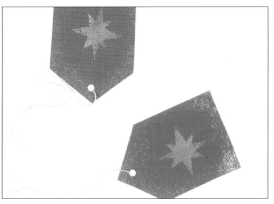

6 Use a hole punch to make a hole for the thread to tie the tag onto the gift.

TISSUE PAPER

Tissue Paper Cards

Tissue paper comes in such a wide range of colours, it is easy to tear and sticks with the minimum of glue. When decorating cards there is no end to the number of ways you can use tissue paper. These cards are made from torn strips of tissue and layered to create blended colours and a simple design. The colours are bright and breezy and very stylish. Have a go at layering colours yourself. Create a natural looking landscape with torn or cut greens, blues and browns.

You will need:

Coloured paper

Tissue paper

Scissors

Glue

1 Fold a piece of coloured paper in half to form the card. Tear off pieces of lime green tissue paper and use small amounts of glue to stick them onto the card.

3 This eyecatching Valentine card is easy to make. You will need to layer 4 pieces of red tissue paper together, fold them in half and carefully tear out a heart shape. The border of the card is made from scissor-cut pieces of red tissue paper.

2 Now layer on strips of pink tissue paper and follow these with a border of blue tissue paper strips. When the glue has set, your card is ready for you to sign and send to a friend.

Index

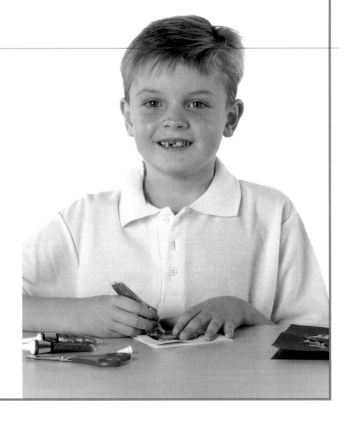